Beneath the Surface

Your hand's a wild creature, bold and spry,
It tickles my ribs, makes me laugh and cry.
In a world of soft whispers, you bring the loud,
With just one poke, I'm lost in the crowd.

A nudge turns my frown into a belly shake,
Like a duck in a pond, I can't help but quake.
Though it starts with a pinch or a playful shove,
I'm tethered to joy, what a silly love!

\

Embracing the Universe

When you grab my hand, it's a cosmic event,
Stars align, and my senses get bent.
It's like the whole galaxy leaned in for a kiss,
A wobbly dance floor, pure comedic bliss.

Your fingers are magic, like spaghetti charms,
They twist and they turn, conjuring laughs and alarms.
In this strange far-off land, let's giggle and twirl,
With a flick of your wrist, you send physics in a whirl!

The Hearth of Touch

Upon my shoulder, your fingers play tricks,
Like squirrels on a wire, teasing with flicks.
Your pat's a warm hug, though it starts as a tease,
Making me chuckle, oh do it, if you please!

The hearth of laughter radiates so bright,
As your fingertips dance, a tickle delight.
Each poke is a wink, a quirk in my day,
In the game of touch, I'm the jester, I say!

Fleeting Glances of Warmth

A nudge on the shoulder, like a quick-firing spark,
It sends my thoughts racing, igniting the dark.
Your laughter's contagious, I'm bubbling with cheer,
Just one little jab, and suddenly, you're near.

In fleeting glances, warmth travels and zips,
From fingertips sweet to joyous little quips.
You spin like a dervish, your joy a bright bloom,
With your playful contact, you light up the room!

Transcendent Connections

When you poke me, it's a spark,
Like a sneeze in the dark.
Your finger taps, I do a jig,
Is that a poke or a loving wig?

With a nudge, my heart takes flight,
A gentle jab, oh what a sight!
Your touch says more than words might prove,
In this dance, we find our groove.

A playful pinch, and I pretend to scold,
But inside I'm laughing, feeling bold.
Each tickle sent, a giggle it follows,
Our little game, like sunny meadows.

So keep on poking, don't stop the fun,
In these moments, we're never done.
Your fingers weave a merry tale,
Together we laugh, we never fail.

Embrace that Lingers

Oh, the way you squeeze me tight,
It's a hug that feels just right.
Like a bear, but with a twist,
In your arms, I can't resist.

Your clumsy grip, a joyful mess,
Leaves me giggling, I must confess.
Like jelly sticks and silly goo,
Each squeeze brings laughter, just me and you.

A tickle here, a playful shove,
We tumble together, it's all in love.
Your warmth wraps 'round, like a cozy scarf,
In this embrace, we make a laugh.

With wobbly arms and silly flails,
We dance through humor, dodging fails.
So let's embrace until the dawn,
In this silliness, our bond lives on.

Electric Embrace

When you poke me, I jump like a cat,
A little zap, a playful spat.
Your fingers wiggle, like they know a dance,
I laugh so hard, caught in a trance.

Static charge, it crackles loud,
We bounce around, giggling proud.
Your touch is like a prankster's call,
Making me stumble, I'm bound to fall.

Each little tickle, a jolt of cheer,
Electric vibes, you're my puppeteer.
With every poke, I giggle and squeal,
Our quirky connection, oh what a deal!

So here we are, in our silly ways,
Creating laughter in endless stay.
Just your fingers, a playful affair,
With each little nudge, I'm lost in air.

Nurturing Fingers

Your fingers dance like they're doing ballet,
Nurturing me in the funniest way.
A gentle poke, then a feather-like tap,
You wrap me in warmth, then spring back, snap!

Soft as butter, yet quick like a wink,
You cradle my heart while making me think.
Your touch is a riddle, tricky to solve,
Like a puzzle game, we happily evolve.

Every pinch comes with a side of glee,
You scalpel my worries, just let me be.
Like a chef with a spoon, taste testers unite,
Your hands are the secret to laughter tonight!

So let's keep spinning these silly tales,
In the land of touches where laughter prevails.
With nurturing fingers, we'll tickle and tease,
Embarking on adventures with absolute ease.

Cherished Caress

Oh, the way you poke with a loving tease,
Each little pinch is a heart-stopping breeze.
Your caress is like bubbles, floating in air,
Bursting with giggles, free of despair.

With a gentle touch, you shake up my mood,
Turning my grumpy into a laughing brood.
You sneak a caress with a cheeky grin,
In this game of touch, I always win!

Like a cat with a laser, I dart to your side,
Each playful nudge is a goofy ride.
Your hands are a bundle of soft-spun dreams,
Wrapping me up in the best of schemes.

So here's to the moments, both funny and bright,
When your cherished caress feels just so right.
Let's dance through the laughter and tickles galore,
In this playful realm, who could ask for more?

Breath of Connection

Your fingers flutter like butterflies roam,
With a single touch, I feel right at home.
Each playful poke, like a firework's flash,
Sparking the laughter, ready to crash.

In the chaos of giggles, our hearts conspire,
Your gentle taps light a friendly fire.
Like two goofy kids on a bright sunny day,
We touch and we laugh, come what may.

Every nudge is a whisper, subtle and sweet,
Creating a rhythm, a dance to our beat.
Your fingers are magic, they can never miss,
A ticklish reminder, a playful bliss.

So here's to the moments we share with such glee,
Your touch brings a smile, oh so carefree.
With each breath of connection, we fall into rhyme,
Having fun together, losing track of time.

Electric Moments

In a crowded room, your hand does tease,
With just a brush, my heart's a breeze.
Like shockwaves dancing on my skin,
Each little nudge invites the grin.

You play the keys of laughter's tune,
With fingertips that make me swoon.
A tickle here, a poke right there,
Each playful jab pulls me to care.

It's magic swirling in the air,
When chaos reigns, you're always fair.
A simple touch, a little jest,
Turns all the fuss into our fest.

So let's embrace this touchy game,
Where things get weird, but that's the fame.
In every pinch and playful poke,
Life's little sparks become our joke.

Heat Beneath the Surface

Your hand finds mine, a candlestick,
Like melted wax with each small flick.
We bake the world with every clasp,
And share giggles over the rasp.

A playful squeeze, the room ignites,
Like popcorn popping on funny nights.
Grab my wrist, a little dance,
Our heat expands with every chance.

I make a joke, you roll your eyes,
But when you touch, it feels so wise.
The warmth we share, a silly trial,
Turns awkward moments to a smile.

Just like a pot that's boiling hot,
Your gentle nudge warms up the spot.
Let's simmer here, don't call it fate,
But let's both laugh and let it bake.

When Hands Speak

A little nudge, a wink, a grin,
Your fingers whisper, let the fun begin.
With each light poke, our laughter flows,
In silent talk, our secret grows.

You tap my shoulder, it's a cue,
That subtle dance, just me and you.
In every squeeze, a silent shout,
Our hands converse without a doubt.

Under tables, little games we play,
A secret signal in a silly way.
Your hand on mine, the world goes mute,
In this funny twist, we both salute.

No words are needed, just the bliss,
Of what our hands say with a kiss.
Like jesters dancing on a stage,
Each touch is humor, we're in a rage.

Shadows of Intimacy

In dim-lit corners, we collide,
Your fingertips tread where secrets hide.
With every slide, a chuckle spills,
In shadows cast, it's laughter that thrills.

We share the light and shade on walls,
Each silly poke, the laughter calls.
Like playful ghosts, we dance unbound,
In whispers soft, our joy is found.

When shadows stretch and flicker bright,
Your touch ignites the teasing light.
In every jab, the world's a show,
Where giggles blaze, and feelings flow.

So here we are, in humor's chase,
Exploring every silly space.
In shadowed realms, where we convene,
Our hands are poets, crafting the scene.

Bound by Gentle Grasp

Your fingers dance like crazy ants,
My hands feel like they've lost their chance.
You squeeze my arm to steal my fries,
And I'm left to contemplate the skies.

A friendly poke, a swift little jab,
Incognito tickles make me drab.
With every pinch, my spirits soar,
How can I stay mad when you want more?

Your playful grip is quite a tease,
Like wrangling cats with the greatest ease.
A nudge, a shove, your cheeky ways,
Make mundane moments a joyful craze.

Through laughter shared and silly grips,
We're caught in this rollercoaster of quips.
Bound by touch, we dance till noon,
With every squeeze, I'm over the moon.

Hands that Heal

Your hands like pizza crust, so cheesy and warm,
Offer comfort during every storm.
A pat on the back, a light little poke,
My troubles vanish like a good joke.

Rub my shoulders? You're quite the pro!
But try to know where not to go.
'Cause if you tickle, chaos will reign,
I'll leap like a cat, screaming in vain!

You paste a band-aid on my broken pride,
While teasing me, you're my loyal guide.
Your sneaky touch has magic defined,
Making bumps and bruises less unkind.

With every pat, I feel the joy,
Like a kid unwrapping their favorite toy.
Your healing hands, they surely rock,
With your warm hug, I feel like a clock!

Symphony of Skin

Your fingers create a merry tune,
Like puppets dancing under the moon.
A gentle poke—what a sweet serenade,
Turning my mood into a fun parade.

A tickle here, a scratch right there,
Like music notes floating in the air.
With every touch, a giggle takes flight,
Syncing our hearts, laughter's pure delight.

Conducting joy, your hands take control,
As we laugh and play, uniting our soul.
A brush on my arm, a swat on the back,
In this silly symphony, we never lack.

With every squeeze, the world fades away,
In this madness, we choose to stay.
Our skin in concert, the fun never ends,
Creating a melody with our silly trends.

Breath of Affection

You blow raspberries while I'm in thought,
Your cheeky charm can't be bought.
A huff, a puff, you're up to your tricks,
Every breath shared, a new comedy mix.

When you hug me tight, I can barely breathe,
It's all in good fun; that's what I believe.
Your playful puffs make my sides ache,
With laughter bursting like a big cupcake.

The lightness of your touch is a grand affair,
Like butterflies buzzing all through the air.
Each snort and squeal adds to the show,
With every breath, our silliness grows.

So let's breathe deeply, my friend of glee,
In this funny circus, just you and me.
Where affection flows like a sparkling drink,
With every touch, our hearts do wink.

Velvet Threads

Soft as a kitten's purr,
Your fingers weave their charm.
Tickles that make me giggle,
You light up with your calm.

Every poke's a tiny zap,
A dance we can't resist.
Like trying to eat soup with chopsticks,
In fun, we coexist.

You touch my cheek like butter,
Making wrinkles, I can't hide.
With every playful jab,
Laughter's found, side by side.

Resonance of Silence

Your hand, a wobbly jello,
Brings echoes to my laughter.
The world falls silent, then boom!
Joy bounces back, faster.

Palms meet in a goofy way,
Like pancakes on a griddle.
Each poke a sweet surprise,
Like finding jelly in the middle.

When you squeeze my silly side,
The room bursts into giggle fits.
With a squish and a pinch,
We play like mischievous knits.

The Alchemy of Contact

Your touch, a chocolate fountain,
Melting laughter everywhere.
Concocting joy in silly ways,
Moments light as air.

Like two magnets, we collide,
In clumsy, funny bliss.
Every poke, a spark ignites,
With every giggling miss.

Swapping high-fives like candy,
Tasting sweetness in the air.
Your mischievous little pinch,
Turns laughter into flare.

Luminous Connection

When you elbow me by chance,
Like fireflies in the night.
A glow of sparkly giggles,
In a radiance so bright.

Your fingers dance like noodles,
Creating chaos galore.
Like balloons with helium,
We float, and then we floor.

In shared silliness we roam,
With touches warm and light.
Each bump and little poke,
Turns laughter into flight.

Unseen Bonds

With just a poke, you bring a grin,
A nudge, a shove, let the laughs begin.
Your finger taps, the chaos stirs,
Who knew a touch could rattle furs?

A high-five here, a pat on the back,
A playful poke, it's a friendly attack.
In silly ways, our spirits lift,
Like magic beans, your touch is a gift.

We twirl and spin, our laughter flows,
Every little nudge, the joy just grows.
With hands that tickle and thumbs that tease,
An unseen bond that brings us to our knees.

So let's embrace this hilarity,
With every poke, we set spirits free.
In playful jabs and giddy winks,
Let's celebrate, as laughter links!

Hands That Heal

A gentle tap upon the head,
You make me giggle 'til I'm red.
A squeeze, a poke, it brings a thrill,
Your quirky touch, my heart to fill.

When life gets tough, and spirits sink,
Your funny jabs, they make me think.
You wave it off, a carefree jest,
In every tickle, you are the best.

A playful slap, a cheeky grin,
Your hands are magic, let the fun begin!
With silly pranks and innocent plays,
You mend my heart in the silliest ways.

So here's to hands that heal the soul,
With every touch, you make me whole.
In laughter's glow, let's make a toast,
To hands of joy, we cherish most!

Embrace of Souls

Your hug's a whirlwind, spins me 'round,
With every squeeze, I'm homeward bound.
In wacky spins and gentle grips,
Our silly antics fuel the quips.

We dance like noodles, all over the place,
Your warm embrace, a silly race.
With tickles here and pokes up there,
We weave our laughs in the funny air.

Like jelly beans that jump and slide,
In every hug, there's joy inside.
So lift me up and let us whirl,
Our souls entwined, like a playful swirl.

With every embrace, our spirits play,
In laughter loved, we'll chase the grey.
So hold me tight, let's twirl and see,
The goofy magic in you and me!

Ripple Effects of Contact

A fingertip flick sends ripples wide,
Your laugh is strong; it's hard to hide.
With every poke, a chuckle grows,
In this funny game, anything goes!

Your playful nudge turns frowns upside down,
A light-hearted tap, I can't wear a frown.
A bump, a hit, we tumble about,
With every laugh, we lose the doubt.

Like stone in a pond, the giggles spread,
Each silly moment, nothing to dread.
With every slap, we make quite the scene,
A wave of joy, it's like we are teens!

So let's keep poking, the fun won't cease,
With every touch, we find our peace.
In this wild dance of giggles and cheer,
The joy in contact, forever near!

Serene Contact

When you poke me on a whim,
I giggle like a child,
Your finger's like a magic wand,
Making all my worries mild.

A gentle nudge upon my arm,
Transforms my frown to glee,
Like tickles from a fluffy cat,
You're the best remedy!

We dance through life with silly taps,
Each touch like a confetti blast,
Your playful jabs bring me to life,
A comedy of joys unsurpassed.

So poke away, oh grab my hand,
With every touch, you make me grin,
Our mutual fun, a grand parade,
In the circus where we both fit in!

Intimacy in Motion

Your elbow gently hits my side,
A weapon of delightful play,
A graze, a shove, a playful nudge,
Who knew we'd laugh this way?

When I lose my balance, wildly sway,
You catch me with a comical flair,
A dance of clumsy twists and turns,
Together, we make quite the pair.

Each poke and prod, a signal clear,
To join the fun, no need to plan,
With every jab, I can't help but cheer,
Your touch turns chaos into a jam!

So let's groove in our silly style,
As fingers dance like feathered quills,
With every touch, you make me smile,
Together is where the humor spills!

Tactile Symphony

A tap upon the shoulder's cue,
Conducts a symphony of glee,
A poke, a pinch, orchestrates joy,
Like music played on a glee spree.

In this duet of silly moves,
Your fingers dance like tiny feet,
With every nudge, our laughter blooms,
Life's rhythm becomes a cheeky beat.

When your hand grazes my cheek, oh dear,
It's a ticket to a playful show,
We giggle through a tactile chorus,
Where every touch makes our spirits grow.

So strum the strings of silly grace,
Let's waltz through each day with cheer,
In this tactile symphony we embrace,
Our funny bond forever near!

Threads of Warmth

A gentle prod, a subtle brush,
Threads of warmth that intertwine,
Like cozy blankets in a rush,
Wrapping us in joy divine.

Your fingers trace a playful line,
Across my arm, they weave and dart,
Each touch a stitch in laughter's quilt,
Creating smiles that light the heart.

In every poke, a friendship blooms,
A tapestry of silly grace,
We'll spin our tales in giggles' rooms,
Our lives stitched close, a warm embrace.

So let your fingers wander free,
Across this quilt of fun we sow,
With each warm thread, just you and me,
In laughter's fabric, we will glow!

Harmony in Our Grip

Your hand in mine, we sway so bold,
Like jellybeans in sunshine, we unfold.
With every squeeze, I feel the blend,
Of laughter lines and joy, on you I depend.

We dance like marionettes, strings in a tangle,
Silly faces, oh, the giggles we wrangle.
A finger poke, a playful jab,
In this touchy game, we both grab.

With every jolt, we spark like fire,
Electric shocks, our hearts aspire.
Your thumbs collide, a happy crash,
Like rubber chickens, we have a splash.

So let's embrace this silly side,
With every poke, there's nowhere to hide.
In the grip of fun, we find our way,
A harmony of laughter, come what may.

Kindred Caresses

In your grin, there's a quirky tease,
Like ticklish feathers carried by the breeze.
Your fingertips, they wiggle, they dance,
Alarming reactions, a chuckling romance.

A peck on the cheek, but oh, what a poke!
We laugh so hard, I nearly choke.
With a playful nudge, your elbow springs,
In this comedy, joy's what it brings.

Each tap, a knot in the shoe of fate,
Hilarity rises, we can't be late.
Like playful puppies in a tug of war,
Kindred souls, together we soar.

With every brush, you make me grin,
A soft pat's the ticket, let the fun begin.
Side by side, we bounce, we flow,
In our caresses, laughter steals the show.

Soulful Clarity through Touch

Each poke you give brings clarity's spark,
Like light bulbs buzzing in the dark.
When you flick my nose, I see the truth,
Connections clearer than a childlike sleuth.

With every pinch, I swear I'm wise,
Your fingers tease, it's no surprise.
A humorous nudge, then life unfolds,
In goofy moments, our story is told.

You poke my side, it tickles my heart,
In this slapstick dance, we play our part.
Thoughts entwined in the laughter's embrace,
Through these playful jabs, I find my place.

So let's waltz along, playful yet shrewd,
In this touchy world, we're never subdued.
With every nudge, clarity shines bright,
Our joyful chuckles, an endless delight.

The Language of Skin

In nudges and prods, our whispers arise,
Conversations spoken without any sighs.
Your elbow rams my ribs in jest,
In this bumpy chat, we're truly blessed.

A finger-stabbed chuckle, a loving poke,
Like soft spaghetti, we wiggle and joke.
With every graze, a language we find,
In silly gestures, our hearts are aligned.

Giggles escape like bubbles in air,
Our skin speaks volumes, without a care.
Each playful hit, a verse we compose,
Language of skin, where laughter flows.

So give me a tap or a funny little crush,
In the silly softness, there's never a rush.
In this crazy chatter, let's carry the tune,
Our slapstick romance, a love that's immune.

Caressing Shadows

In the park, we dance like fools,
Tickling shadows, breaking rules.
Your fingers poke, a playful tease,
Spooking squirrels, rustling leaves.

We laugh out loud, the sunlight beams,
Chasing dreams in childlike themes.
A gentle nudge, my hat's askew,
Oh, how I love this silly view!

With every touch, a giggle comes,
You squish my cheeks, oh, how it hums!
We snatch the clouds, we're quite the pair,
Your playful swat sends me in the air.

We bump our arms on the park bench,
You shove my snacks, you little wrench!
A tickle fight, we bob and weave,
Laughter shared, in joy we believe.

Intimate Threads of Fate

You threw a wink that pulled my heart,
With just a touch, we're off the chart.
Our fingers crossed like tangled yarn,
Each squeeze a spell, a quirky charm.

You flick my ear, I playfully shove,
Caught in threads of mischief and love.
We weave our joys, with knots so tight,
That even hiccups become delight.

You poke my side, I squeal in glee,
Your silly antics, they rescue me.
We spin around like tops in flight,
Living in laughter, hearts so light.

A nudge here, a poke right there,
We dance through life without a care.
In this game of jocular fate,
Bring out the fun, let's celebrate!

A Touch of Sunlight

You reach for me like morning rays,
Brightening up my clumsy ways.
Your nudges come with sunny grins,
Chasing away the dull life spins.

With a playful jab, my drink you spill,
We burst with laughter, what a thrill!
You copy cats, you silly tease,
I'm giggling hard, I can't find ease.

When you touch my arm, I fly away,
A comedic twist to brighten the day.
You steal the sun with every flair,
I tumble, roll, and forget my care.

Your playful wrist flicks magic sparks,
A radiant dance laced with fun arcs.
Together we're a dazzling sight,
With each warm touch, the world feels right.

The Weight of Affection

Your poke's a feather, oh so light,
But makes me giggle with delight.
You plop a hug like a clumsy bear,
With every squeeze, I can't help but stare.

You bounce around, a rubber ball,
A gentle nudge, it's pure enthrall.
We trip and stumble, dance just so,
With every step, our laughter grows.

Your hand a pillow, soft and warm,
With each goofy move, we weather the storm.
The weight of love, it feels just right,
In this playful waltz, we shine bright.

Your silly jokes, a tickling breeze,
We wobble and giggle, drop to our knees.
With every moment, let joy ascend,
For with your touch, my heart you mend.

Fluid Bonds

Your fingers dance like little kids,
They tickle me, oh what a bid!
In this giggle-filled parade,
We shake the world, let's not be afraid.

The way you poke, the way you squeeze,
Turns awkward moments into a breeze.
Your touch has charm, your touch has flair,
Like jellybeans flying through the air.

Oh, how your nudges make me snort,
In this delightful, playful sport.
With every prod, I start to grin,
Our laughter bubbles—let the fun begin!

So let's keep poking, let's have a blast,
With silly touches, we'll hold fast.
A whimsical bond, both sweet and bright,
Our funny frolic's a glorious sight!

Sensory Traces

A poke here and a tickle there,
Your playful swipes fill the air.
Like fluffy clouds on a sunny day,
You buzz my senses in a crazy way.

Your fingertips bring sparks and flare,
Each gentle nudge leads me to dare.
Like spaghetti strands, we twist and twine,
In our fun mess, everything's fine!

From silly pinches to playful slaps,
We navigate our laughter gaps.
Your playful nudges, they boost my cheer,
Creating joy that's loud and clear.

In this game of sensory delight,
Our chuckles dance through day and night.
With every touch, we create a song,
In this funny world, we truly belong!

Kisses in the Air

A peck on the cheek, a playful nudge,
You make me laugh, I'm never judged.
With every kiss blown from afar,
You turn my grump into a star!

Your lips like feathers brush my face,
A tickly whirlwind, such a race.
I chase these kisses through the room,
And dodge your goofy magic bloom!

With a wink and a cheeky smile,
You make monotony feel worthwhile.
In this comical chase, we fly,
Kissing the air, oh my, oh my!

So let's blow kisses, high and low,
In our whirlwind of fun, we glow.
Funny moments stacked like gold,
In this love, we never grow old!

Molten Affection

Your hugs ignite a giggly spark,
Like lava lamps dancing in the dark.
You squeeze me tight, then let me go,
A molten hug, what a fun show!

Cuddly warmth, it's pure delight,
We tumble about in silly flight.
Your jiggly affection's a sight to see,
Like jelly rolling, so carefree!

You smother me with laughter's flame,
In our touch-game, we're never tame.
With every quirk and silly glance,
We twist and twirl in our sweet romance.

So let's keep melting, warm and bright,
In this joy-ride of silly light.
Molten laughter, hugs galore,
With every touch, I love you more!

The Language We Share

Your hand on mine speaks volumes,
With every poke and every squeeze.
It's like we're two cartoon characters,
Fighting over the last piece of cheese.

A playful nudge, a soft embrace,
Turns my worries into giggles,
Each palm is a little translator,
Making love speak through silly wiggles.

In a world of loud discussions,
Our silence is a funny dance.
A raised eyebrow or a quick poke,
Turns the mundane into romance.

With just a touch, you say so much,
Like cats who fight but love the same.
We share a language made of smiles,
Never needing to play the blame.

Sparks in Silence

When fingers brush, a spark ignites,
A jolt like coffee, pure delight.
I swear I saw your hair stand tall,
Was it magic, or just a sprawl?

Our secret code of fleeting touches,
Turns handshakes into marching huddles.
With every poke, the laughter doubles,
Creating joy, and friend-filled cuddles.

We're like two cats upon a wire,
One misstep and we both conspire.
But with that slip, there comes the play,
And all our worries drift away.

So every nudge holds untold tales,
Of mischief shared on lopsided scales.
In our world of funny laughter,
You're the punchline I chase after.

Friction of Heartstrings

When you tap my shoulder just for fun,
It sings like a string when plucked just right.
Each tap's a giggle, a friendly pun,
Drawing a smile that's out of sight.

Our fingers dance like stars at night,
Creating sparks, both soft and bright.
A funny slip that makes us laugh,
Reveals a bond that's quite the craft.

You steal my popcorn with a grin,
And all my snacks, they just vanish in.
Your touch ignites a silly feud,
Turning popcorn fights into good mood.

With every poke and playful shove,
We banter like kids, chasing our love.
The friction pulls at heartstrings tight,
While laughter echoes through the night.

Caress of the Cosmos

Your fingers twirl, like galaxies round,
Making stars appear where none were found.
A tickle here, a poke right there,
In this universe, we're quite the pair.

Each touch is a note in a cosmic song,
Taking the mundane and making it strong.
Like dancing comets, we swirl and sway,
In the gravity of laughter, we play away.

Tickling dreams, you spark delight,
Like playful aliens in the night.
With every caress, hearts intertwine,
Creating galaxies that truly shine.

So let's orbit around with joy and cheer,
Navigating this world, my dear.
In the cosmos of giggles, let's forever touch,
For in this dance, I love you so much.

Vibration of Affection

Your fingers glide like feathers light,
Sending giggles, it's pure delight.
A poke here, a tickle there,
Silly laughter fills the air.

In your grasp, my worries fade,
A gentle squeeze, my worries played.
You wave a hand like casting spells,
Jokes erupt where affection dwells.

With every nudge, sparks of glee,
Your playful jabs, they set me free.
You juggle warmth with a wink or two,
Creating smiles, just us two.

Each pat and poke, a comic art,
Shaping laughter straight from the heart.
In this dance of silly bliss,
Your touch, my dear, is pure happiness.

Orbit of Tenderness

Come spin with me in joy's embrace,
Your playful nudges, a merry chase.
A flick, a giggle, we swerve and twirl,
In this orbit, my heart does whirl.

Your palm a beacon, warmth so clear,
A light pat sends me soaring here.
In circles drawn by witty swats,
Every bump a comedic plot.

We bounce around, a joyful ride,
Each poke a thrill, a swinging tide.
Your touch like jelly, soft and sweet,
In this dance, we can't be beat.

So take my hand, let's whirl away,
With silly moments that brightly play.
In this embrace of jerky fun,
Tender orbit—just us, the chosen one.

Heartfelt Imprints

Your fingertips, they leave a trace,
A tickle dance across my face.
Like little whispers on my skin,
Each mark a joke where love begins.

In playful jabs, I find my cheer,
Funny moments, my heart steers clear.
With every touch, a story spun,
Your giggles twinkle, my favorite pun.

A gentle poke, oh how it sings,
Each laugh a gift, my heart it brings.
You leave your prints on me so light,
Shaping joy in the dead of night.

So here we are, a duo bold,
With heartfelt imprints, tales untold.
Through laughter's lens, together we clutch,
These tender marks, your loving touch.

Streams of Comfort

Your hands like rivers smoothly glide,
Bringing laughter, warmth beside.
A gentle nudge, a playful shove,
Together we float in giggles of love.

In streams of joy, we wade and flow,
With splashes of jokes that wildly grow.
A playful natter to ease the day,
Your touch the current leading the way.

Each little tickle, a buoyant wave,
Your laughter lifts me, always saves.
We paddle through moments, bright and fun,
In this river, we both are one.

So let the waters pull us near,
In this stream, a joyful cheer.
With every touch, together we sail,
Finding comfort in our laugh-filled tale.

Glimpse of the Soul

Your fingers dance like ants on fire,
They wiggle and squirm, lift me higher.
A poke, a nudge, a playful tease,
My giggles escape like buzzing bees.

In a world of hugs and tickling darts,
Your simple touch can mend small parts.
Like a light switch flicked, I shout, "Hooray!"
My heart's a flurry in a humorous sway.

Be it a poke or a gentle prod,
With every touch, I find it odd.
A seemingly innocent jest ignites,
A laugh erupts in fuzzy delights.

So as we frolic and let joy soar,
With every touch, I crave more and more.
For in this fun, our spirits brawl,
A quirky dance, a laugh for all.

The Brush of Destiny

Your fingertips, like feathers, play,
They twist and twirl, in wild array.
Each gentle brush invites a grin,
Like tickling grass or a playful spin.

When you poke my side, oh what a sound,
An unexpected squeal, hilariously found.
Two laughs collide, like cats in a race,
Every touch a spark, a comical chase.

Eureka moments crafted in jest,
Your brush of fate is truly the best.
Like silly putty molding a thought,
In this goofy ballet, joy is caught.

So let's keep touching, let humor win,
For with each encounter, we both grin.
In the fabric of laughter, our fates entwine,
In this delightful dance, everything's fine.

Unspoken Affection

Your gentle tap is a comedy show,
Fingers play tricks that steal the glow.
Each playful poke, a silent cue,
In every elbow jab, I laugh with you.

Thoughts left unsaid weave in our dance,
Every touch a wink, every poke a chance.
We're a duo of giggles with love on display,
Turning innocent brushes into wild play.

Like sneaky whispers, our fingers tease,
A laugh erupts, and my heart's at ease.
For with each unspoken little jest,
Your gentle taps put humor to the test.

So let's keep flirting with a silly touch,
In this game of giggles, I like you much.
Together we create mischief and glee,
An unspoken bond, just you and me.

Veil of Touch

With a gentle nudge, you break the air,
Your fingertips play like they just don't care.
Each prodding poke is a master plan,
To crack me up in this lively jam.

Like a feather falling on a sleepy cat,
Your touch awakens my happy spat.
We're a pair of jesters, don't you see?
In this game of tickles, we're silly as can be.

Your fingertips whisper secrets in jest,
Hoping to catch me off-guard, no rest.
With every brush and sly little tease,
Laughter erupts, like popping cheese.

So let's keep touching with glee and flair,
In this comedic dance, we're a perfect pair.
Through the veil of humor, our spirits ignite,
With each little poke, we take off in flight.

Dance of the Ques

In the kitchen, pots do sway,
As I dance, they beg me to play.
With spatula acts, I flip and twirl,
Surely, this rhythm's a culinary whirl.

The dog joins in, a furry delight,
With tail-wagging moves that feel just right.
My cat throws shade, thinks I'm a fool,
Yet here I am, grooving like I rule.

Neighbors peek, with a laugh or two,
As my kitchen floor becomes a zoo.
Quesadillas sizzling, my feet have their say,
In this wacky dance, I won't decay.

Tacos on plates and chips in hand,
Dinner party chaos, isn't it grand?
The quest for fun, oh what a scene,
Next time, they'll join—if only they're keen!

Embrace of Euphoria

In the hallway, a hug's in flight,
Cousin's warm grin, it feels just right.
A clumsy clasp, we wobble and sway,
Like a pair of balloons, we float away.

A ticklish poke, and I burst into glee,
Laughter erupts, just you and me.
We wobble like jellies, what a sight,
Euphoria blooms on a Sunday night.

With popcorn clouds that dance in the air,
As we hug it out, banishing despair.
Our hearts do cha-cha, twirling around,
In silly embraces, true joy is found.

In this joyful mess, we're lost in the cheer,
The hugs get tighter as friends draw near.
Embraces of laughter, like candy so sweet,
Who knew happiness came with two left feet?

Whispers of Connection

Beneath the moon, two fingers entwine,
In this soft glow, our giggles align.
A secret shared, like candy on lips,
Our whispers float, like mischievous nips.

With a nudge and a poke, we spark the night,
Every word thrown makes everything light.
Witty banter sails through the breeze,
Like two goofballs, we're lost with ease.

The stars above twinkle with glee,
As our laughter connects, just you and me.
In this cosmic game, we twirl and trance,
What began as a whisper turned into a dance.

So let's keep this moment tucked in our hearts,
With each silly joke, true magic starts.
For in these whispers, both loud and profound,
We find our connection in fun all around!

Elegance in Our Embrace

In a dress that spins, I take my stance,
Awkward moves, but oh what a chance!
Our arms intertwine in a wobbly spin,
Who knew elegance could wear such a grin?

With two left feet, we shuffle about,
And our laughter, oh my, it leaves no doubt.
Like a dance of penguins, we strut and sway,
How can clumsiness steal joy away?

A graceful dip becomes a fumble and fall,
Yet here we are, laughing through it all.
In exquisite chaos, we find our grace,
As elegant hugs keep us from space.

With every embrace, a new tale we weave,
Amidst all the giggles, we choose to believe.
Elegance thrives in this silly race,
In blooms of laughter, we find our place.

The Fabric of Affection

In a world made of hugs and threads,
We stitch love into our beds.
With giggles and laughter, we twist and twine,
Making blankets of joy, oh how they shine!

The fabric's a bit worn, with holes here and there,
But each snag is a story we lovingly share.
A patchwork of moments, both silly and sweet,
In this quilt of affection, life's a joyful treat!

So grab a needle, let's mend what we've got,
Our hearts in the sewing basket, tied up in knots.
With each playful stitch, our bond strengthens anew,
In this crazy old quilt, it's always me and you!

When the world feels frayed and a little off course,
We wrap up together, a cozy discourse.
With smiles we'll gather, a patchwork parade,
In the fabric of affection, love will never fade!

Elysian Caress

A gentle poke or just a nudge,
Turns mundane moments into a judge.
Your touch is a tickle, a warm embrace,
Makes me giggle, feels like a race!

With fingers that dance like bees on the run,
You create a buzz—a riot of fun!
A ruffle here, a playful jab there,
In this merry game, we have little care!

When you flick my ear or wriggle my toes,
A symphony of laughter is how our joy grows.
Each playful poke, a secret delight,
In this waltz of whimsy, we twirl into night!

Oh, these jolly moments, they sweep me away,
A lighthearted frolic in the bright of the day.
With every caress, we craft a new dance,
In the laughter of life, we find our romance!

Dances of Desire

Two hands collide, a clumsy twirl,
In this ballet, hearts jitter and whirl.
With every slip, giggles abound,
In our wobbly waltz, love's joy is found!

A tap on the shoulder, a tickle on the side,
Makes our awkward movement a gleeful ride.
In this dance of delight, we spin and we sway,
Inventing new steps to brighten the day!

You lead with a grin, I follow with flair,
With backdrop of laughter, who's counting? We dare!
Our feet might get tangled, but who's keeping score?
In this fun-loving frolic, we keep asking for more!

So let's shake our bones, let's jive, let's jump,
In the rhythm of joy, it's a jubilant thump.
With each clumsy step, we'll always ignite,
In this dance of our hearts, the world feels just right!

Handprints on the Heart

Your fingers leave marks that tell a tale,
With smudges of joy, we'll never fail.
A splash of affection, like paint on a wall,
Each handprint reminds us to always stand tall!

From high-fives to hugs, we make our own signs,
A canvas of laughter, where happiness shines.
Like little love letters, your fingerprints show,
Our hearts are a gallery where good vibes flow!

With every soft touch, a masterpiece grows,
In this art of affection, love never slows.
So let's color outside the lines, what a mess!
In this joyful exhibit, who needs to impress?

With handprints that shimmer in all of our hues,
We'll dance through our days and create what we choose.
In the gallery of life, let's paint our own chart,
With joy and with laughter, just handprints on heart!

Melody in Movement

Your fingers dance like they're alive,
Spinning tales that make me thrive.
A tap, a poke, a playful shove,
In this rhythm, we're in love.

When you tickle, I squeal with glee,
A symphony made just for me.
The clumsy jive and silly sway,
We groove together day by day.

Hands that Speak

Your hands tell jokes without a word,
They wiggle, twist, and sometimes hurt.
With a gentle push or a soft squeeze,
You have a knack that aims to please.

A wave goodbye, or a cheeky grin,
Those palm high-fives are sure to win.
Like magic wands, they conjure smiles,
With flailing thumbs and goofy styles.

Touching Moments

Oh, that nudge, a gentle poke,
Turns my frown into a joke.
A slap on the back or a pat on the head,
In this playful dance, no tears are shed.

Your playful pinches spark delight,
In every touch, everything feels right.
We giggle, we wiggle, just having fun,
In a silly world where we both run.

Vibrations of Love

Your touch is like a wacky tune,
That bounces around like a happy balloon.
From high-fives to thumbs-up cheers,
You amplify my goofy fears.

A little jab, a butterfingers drop,
Together we'll dance till we pop!
With every tap, a giggle breaks,
Vibrations rise, just for laughs' sake.

Caressing Currents

A gentle poke, a playful nudge,
Your fingers tease, can't hold a grudge.
They tickle toes and pinch my side,
A whirlwind laugh, let's take a ride!

In every swipe, a whirlwind spin,
Your touch ignites the fun within.
A slapstick dance, we twirl around,
In this madcap joy, we're truly bound.

With smiling hands, you toss a snack,
A sugary treat, do I lack?
With each small prod, my spirits soar,
Your touch is magic, who could want more?

Let's frolic through this playful haze,
With every jab, we spark a blaze.
In giggles shared, no need for fuss,
Together in fun, just you and us.

Gentle Sparks of Affection

A playful poke, a twitchy tease,
Your fingertips dance with such ease.
A pinch, a prod, a cheeky grin,
In the game of life, we both win.

You wave your hands like a tiny breeze,
They tickle my neck, they strive to please.
With each small touch a giggle ensues,
It's like we've crafted our own funny muse.

Your hands flutter like a silly bird,
Spreading joy, just like I heard.
A tap on the shoulder, a nudge or a fuss,
In this circus of love, it's a plus!

With every jab, I laugh and squirm,
Your playful touch confirms the term.
In the rollercoaster of our days,
We ride the highs in delightful ways.

Echoes of a Loving Hand

A light pinch here, a gentle jab,
Your playful teasing is quite the fab.
From playful swats to soft, sweet pats,
My heart does flipping acrobatics!

Like echoes bouncing off the wall,
Your touch sends shivers, I'm having a ball.
With every poke, there's laughter near,
In this crazy dance, I hold you dear.

A loving nudge when I look unwell,
Or just a poke to bet you can't tell.
Those funny quirks, they steal my breath,
With every touch, you conquer death.

In tickles and prods, our spirits collide,
Your hand, my compass, my joyful guide.
Together we stand, in laughter we bloom,
With echoes of love that light up the room.

The Dance of Fingertips

In the dance of fingers, we twirl and spin,
Each tickle and touch sends joy within.
A gentle prod, a comical shove,
Your fingertips whisper the language of love.

With every little playful poke,
You're the reason I giggle and choke!
A slap on the back, a quick silly tease,
You turn my frown into giggly ease.

Your hands, they shimmy like no other,
Funny gestures that make me smother.
A gentle touch just makes my day,
In this silly waltz, we laugh and play.

So let's swirl around till the night is done,
With silly touches we have our fun.
In this dance of hands, we feel alive,
In our funny rhythm, we truly thrive.

Sculpted by Touch

Fingers dance like playful gnomes,
They shape the air, like pizza dough.
A poke, a prod, it's all in fun,
Who knew a pat could steal a show?

Like a silent mime with hands so sly,
Each poke a joke, each nudge a laugh.
You're crafting smiles, oh my oh my,
Like sculpting art from a photograph.

With every brush upon the skin,
A tickle here, a squeeze right there.
Guess touch can make the shyest grin,
Like a feathered tickle, oh so rare!

So let's just touch and make it sweet,
Your fingers know just how to tease.
In this funny dance, we can't be beat,
For laughter's magic is sure to please.

Ballad of the Heart's Reach

A swat on the back, a pat on the head,
You just can't help but play around.
Each poke and prod is just so widespread,
Go ahead, be silly, don't hold the sound!

Like a rubber band that wants to snap,
You touch with purpose, oh what a skill!
A pinch, a tug, you set the trap,
Turning normal days into a thrill!

Each jab and jabber, like jesters' fun,
You pull my heart like a funny string.
Every little nudge, it weighs a ton,
But oh, what laughter that it can bring!

So let's rejoice in this playful dance,
With every bump, we make a stride.
A delightful moment or a silly chance,
Together, let the giggles collide!

Unwritten Scripts

In a world of scripts we never write,
Your fingers hold the ink, so true.
With a jab, a poke, you spark delight,
Page by page, it's all about you!

Every touch, a scene, a funny plot,
Who knew a tickle could inspire?
In this unwritten script, we tie the knot,
Making a rib-tickling empire!

The dialogue flows from every squeeze,
Oh, the laughter that fills the air!
With every touch, you bring me to knees,
Shaking with joy, you've got that flair!

So let's keep scribbling, no need for pens,
With giggles in our hearts, we'll play.
This comic tale just never ends,
In the book of fun, we'll find our way.

Tides of Emotion

With every wave, your fingers tease,
A splash of joy, they dance and glide.
They pull me in, like ocean breeze,
Where funny moments reside!

Each poke a wave, each tickle deep,
Riding this current, oh what a ride!
We stumble and laugh, no need for sleep,
In the tide of giggles, we'll abide.

The shore of smiles is close at hand,
With every touch, our hearts unite.
In this sea of laughter, understand,
We're sailing vessels, full of light!

So let the waves keep crashing near,
With playful splashes on the way.
In this tide of joy, let's have no fear,
Together, we'll surf the funny spray.

The Art of Holding

With arms like octopus, I wrap you tight,
A squeeze so fierce, it gives you a fright.
You giggle and wiggle, try to break free,
But my grip's a treasure, you'd better agree.

In crowded rooms, I'm like a clingy vine,
A friendly hug, with a dash of divine.
You know it's awkward, yet silly and fun,
My hugs are like cookies—too good to shun!

The way we embrace, a zany ballet,
Round and round, in the silliest way.
You peek over shoulders, roll your eyes too,
But deep in your heart, you love this zoo!

So here's to our antics, our hug-a-thon,
In this wacky dance, we both can't go wrong.
No need for the gym, we've found our own way,
With laughter and joy, we seize the day!

Touching the Infinite

In every poke, a small spark ignites,
A tickle here, it's pure delight!
You swat and laugh, a playful retreat,
Like butterflies dancing, our hands meet.

Fingers collide, like magnets in play,
You tease with your elbow, 'Hey, not today!'
But I'm just getting started, oh what a show,
In this circus of touch, there's more fun to flow.

The brush of our hands, a cosmic affair,
Like ketchup on fries, it's meant to be shared.
With giggles and silly faces we play,
What a strange world, where we fumble away!

In the realm of high fives and tickling stunts,
We'll reach for the stars, do playful runs.
So let's stretch our fingers, let's feel the vibe,
In this joyful dance, we shall thrive!

Sensing the Unspoken

There's magic in silence, a squeeze we both know,
A nudge to the elbow, a friendly hello.
With knowing glances and playful jabs,
We communicate secrets like silly old brabs.

You poke my sides when the joke goes too far,
While rolling your eyes, you giggle like a star.
A simple gesture, no words need arise,
In the dance of our touch, we find the surprise.

Like fingers that trace, a map drawn in jest,
Each tickle a treasure, a soft little test.
You read my mind with your playful touch,
In this world of laughter, it's never too much.

So let's keep this game, this quirky ballet,
In the winks and the nudges, we'll find our way.
With each little gesture, let joy be a spark,
Our silent connection, a joyful hallmark!

Caress of Kindred Spirits

Our fingers intertwine like vines on a wall,
A playful embrace defying the fall.
With each gentle poke, a giggle ensues,
In the garden of friendship, there's no room for blues.

We nudge and we poke, like children at play,
A tap on the shoulder, much brighter than day.
With laughter and antics, we dance through the air,
In the caress of the moment, we shed every care.

Witty exchanges, a tug here and there,
A nudge on your hip, you pretend not to care.
But we share a secret, a bond so sincere,
In the joy of our laughter, we've nothing to fear.

So let's keep on poking, and squeezing with glee,
In this merry journey, just you and me.
Together like spirit, our touch is the key,
Unlocking the fun, forever carefree!

Ethereal Embrace

When fingertips dance like silly sprites,
They lift my spirits to dizzying heights.
A gentle poke and a playful shove,
It's like we're part of a comedy of love.

With each little nudge, a giggle is brewed,
Falling like clowns, oh how absurd!
Rubber chicken hands and wiggly arms,
Your silly touch disarms me with charms.

Our palms collide in a slapstick spree,
I swear you've mastered the art of spree!
A tickle here, a pat in the head,
With laughter echoing, we dance instead.

So let our fingers pull some stunts,
A few high-fives, and silly grunts.
In this joyful game, two hearts entwine,
Magic happens every time you're mine.

Skin Deep Harmony

Your skin finds mine in a playful jest,
Like spaghetti noodles, we're tangled and blessed.
With a boop on the nose and a wink in the air,
Our fingers tango without a care.

Slaps and tickles, it's quite the delight,
We giggle and squirm in this playful fight.
A rush of laughter, quick as a flash,
Your wink makes my heart do a cartoonish crash.

Each touch a melody, silly and sweet,
The symphony thrives in this playful beat.
We hop and we giggle, oh what a scene,
Like a zany cartoon, we're living the dream.

So here's to the antics, the whimsical fun,
In this skin-deep dance, we're never outdone.
Let's mash our fingers and skip with delight,
In this hullabaloo, we could dance all night.

Fragrance of Contact

When your hand greets mine, it's a comical dream,
Like a whiff of pizza topped with whipped cream.
A clap and a grin, a tickle in return,
In this fun-filled circus, our laughter does churn.

Your playful punches, soft as a cloud,
Wrap me in warmth, where joy is loud.
A funny clench and a quick tickle spree,
Oh, the fragrance of laughter, just you and me.

A high five erupts, our fingers entwine,
Like sneaky little elves, so silly but fine.
Every brush of skin, a whimsical song,
It's a riotous dance where we both belong.

So here in this arena, our bodies collide,
In the fragrance of contact, let giggles abide.
A swirl of delight, oh what a perfect match,
In this humorous balmy, we'll never detach.

Tender Collisions

With every collision, we bounce and we sway,
Your pokes spark a giggle that's here to stay.
It's a whirlwind of fun, a slapstick affair,
Where touches and chuckles dance in the air.

The poke in the ribs that tickles me so,
With a shy little grin, your antics steal the show.
Like a pair of clowns, we tumble and fall,
In this tender comedy, we have a ball.

A light-hearted squeeze that sets off a spree,
Of laughter and joy, oh just wait and see!
We trip on joy and skip on a plea,
In this charmingly silly, perfect harmony.

So let's collide like cushions in flight,
With every sweet poke, we ignite the night.
In this wacky dance of ferocious glee,
Your gentle touch is the punchline for me.

Soft Echoes of Care

A poke on the arm, oh what a delight,
You giggle and squirm, it's quite the sight.
A gentle nudge here, a playful shove,
Who knew a little touch could feel like love?

A tickle on ribs, a pinch on the cheek,
Our laughter erupts, words barely can speak.
In this silly dance, we sway and we leap,
With every small touch, the secrets we keep.

High fives exchanged, claps echo like song,
In our playful world, nothing feels wrong.
A pat on the back, a nudge in the ribs,
Through our playful antics, connection jibs!

So here's to the touches, both funny and light,
A squish of the cheeks makes everything bright.
In laughter we find, oh what a fresh start,
Soft echoes of care, forever our art.

The Pulse of Connection

A tap on the shoulder, oh what a tease,
You jump and you giggle, just like a breeze.
In the crowd, a wink, perhaps a light poke,
It's not just a touch, it's the laughter we stoke.

With each playful shove, our spirits take flight,
Dance moves ensue, oh what a sight!
Like rubbery friends, we bounce and we sway,
Every light jab brings a smile to our day.

A nudge with a finger or a tap on the knee,
Turns mundane moments to pure comedy.
In the rhythm of laughter, our hearts intertwine,
With every small touch, your joy is divine!

So let's keep it going, this funny display,
Of jests and of giggles, come join in the play.
Your touch is a spark, igniting the zest,
In the pulse of connection, we truly are blessed.

Caressed by Destiny

A brush of the hand, oh what a delight,
You turn with a grin, your eyes shining bright.
In our silly game, fate gives us a nudge,
With each little poke, we simply will budge.

A playful whirl, and a slip on the floor,
A bump into you, leaves me wanting more.
In tossing of pillows, or a friendly shove,
Destiny chuckles, it's all made of love.

Your side-slap of laughter, oh don't make me fall,
Every snicker and touch, it's the best of them all.
From lighthearted jabs to each ticklish dare,
We're caressed by this fate, the world feels so rare.

So let's keep it zany, together we thrive,
With silly affection, we both come alive.
In the chaos of joy, forever we'll be,
Caressed by this journey, just you and me.

Imprints of Togetherness

A swift poke to the ribs, it's a childish game,
You shout and you laugh, oh what a shame!
With each little jab, our spirits combine,
Imprints of joy weave a bond so divine.

A shared silly dance, arms flailing around,
In a world full of giggles, our joy knows no bound.
In playful exchanges like the pat on a back,
We leave little markers along our own track.

A nudge on your side, an elbow in play,
With each punchy jest, we light up the day.
The warmth of your smile, like sunshine it glows,
In this tapestry woven, togetherness grows.

So let's cherish the moments that bring us delight,
In these cute little antics, our hearts take flight.
With every soft hit, let the laughter resound,
In the imprints we make, true joy can be found.

Whispers of Connection

Your fingers dance like tiny mice,
Tickling truths that feel so nice.
A playful poke, a gentle nudge,
In this light banter, we won't budge.

With every tap, a giggle shared,
A secret friend who never cared.
We wriggle, wiggle, laugh, and shout,
In silly games, we swirl about.

Echoes Beneath Our Skin

A playful poke, you made me squeal,
Like ticklish spots, oh what a deal!
You swipe my arm, I jump in fright,
But laughter bounces back, so light.

We set the stage, a slapstick show,
Your touch ignites a jolly glow.
With every touch, there's no retreat,
In our mishaps, life is sweet.

Rippled Embrace

Your hand gave mine a little tease,
Like a gentle breeze through autumn leaves.
We laugh and twirl, a merry spree,
Our touches start a grand jubilee.

The jests we make, the pranks we play,
In this touchy ballet, we sway.
A poke, a prod, a friendly slap,
Together in mischief, we overlap.

Fingertips of Fate

Your poke on my side, a swift surprise,
Caught off guard, I blink my eyes.
A tickle here, a playful shove,
In every touch, we find our love.

We twirl around like stars in flight,
Turning simple times to pure delight.
With every jab, a smile is found,
In this merry dance, we twirl around.

Unseen Currents

In the room, there's a dance, a sway,
Every poke and prod makes me laugh away.
A tickle here, a nudge there,
Our giggles merge like a wild affair.

With every pat, a shockwave grows,
As if we're sparks from a jolt of prose.
A playful jab turns serious quick,
These silly moves are quite the trick!

Remember that time with a playful squeeze?
You made me giggle, brought me to my knees.
A smirk, a grin, we roll on the floor,
Who knew soft touches would lead to this roar?

So keep your pokes and wiggly twists,
In our goofy dance of fluttery fists.
In invisible waves, the joy is vast,
Your playful touch makes my heart beat fast!

Tender Imprints

A gentle tap upon my back,
Turns my thoughts into a silly snack.
With every squeeze, my worries cease,
Your silly pokes bring me such peace.

A little nudge, a playful push,
Like secret notes in a lover's hush.
We dance around like kids at play,
Leaving fingerprints that never fray.

Your fingers tickle, my sides they ache,
In this tender game of fun we make.
A messy hug, a wobbly grin,
In every touch, our laughter spins.

So here's to the moments when fingers collide,
Southern charm make our joy abide.
With every brush, we create a spark,
In this wild dance, let's leave a mark!

Texture of Longing

A caress that swirls like cream in tea,
With every touch, I just can't flee.
Fingertips weave a playful spell,
As we giggle and snicker, it's clear, all's well.

Your poke sends ripples across my skin,
Silly sensations where we begin.
Each playful jab, a whisper shared,
In these textures, nothing's spared.

A soft nudge, quite out of the blue,
My heart does flips, just like a kangaroo.
In this crazy blend of fun and jest,
Your tender touch is simply the best!

So let's frolic in this tactile game,
Each tap and wag, never the same.
In the dance of silliness, we'll find our way,
With every little touch, we laugh and sway!

Pulse of Togetherness

Your little jabs make time freeze,
Bursting laughter with playful ease.
Like a heartbeat in a rhythm divine,
Our antics twirl, oh what a sign!

Each push and pull, a slapstick scene,
Creating memories thick and keen.
In the whirlwind of touches, a spark ignites,
We're partners in this joyful flight!

With every poke, we draw a line,
In this silly game, you're truly fine.
Nonsense flows from our fingertips,
In this pulse of laughter, we're soulmates, no scripts!

So let's embrace this wiggly twine,
With every tickle, let our hearts align.
For when you touch, the world seems right,
In our fun-filled dance, we'll take flight!

Connections Woven in Touch

Your finger stayed on my ketchup,
It slid away like a sneaky pup.
With laughter shared and fries in a heap,
Our greasy hands made memories deep.

A high-five gone wrong, what a sight!
A slap on the back—oh, what a fright!
We tangled our fingers in silly pretzels,
Laughing so hard, our belly's an wrestle.

Sticky glue stuck on my shoe,
A circus of chaos, just me and you.
With every poke comes a playful cheer,
The fun in the tactile, oh dear, oh dear!

In our goofy grip, we find delight,
Handfuls of giggles, what a sweet night.
So let's embrace this silly way,
In the warm of our touch, we forever play.

Threads of Serenity

Your hand on my shoulder, a ticklish tease,
Like whispers of comfort, a gentle breeze.
We dance through the kitchen, the plants all sway,
With laughter as spices, we sauté our day.

Finger painting smiles on the kitchen wall,
A splash of orange, I may just fall!
Our messy creations bring joy and fun,
In the tapestry of chaos, we've hardly just begun.

A squeeze on the cheek, oh what a grin,
In our soft embrace, life's where we begin.
With every touch, the laughter grows,
In this web of joy, our friendship flows.

So here's to the silly, embrace the crook,
Let's write our stories with every nook.
With threads of fun and brave little stunts,
We weave a life that forever confronts.

The Softest Echo

Tickles in the air, as we sit side by side,
A gentle poke leading our giggle tide.
Your smile, a spark, and a nudge set it free,
Echoes of laughter, as soft as can be.

A pillow fight turns into comedy hour,
With marshmallow fluff, what a sweet power!
In whispers of warmth, we playfully chuckle,
As soft little touches make hearts do a shuffle.

Expectations of calm? Let's toss them away!
With chaos akin to a frolicking ballet.
Each pinch of your hand, a joyful surprise,
In echoes so soft, our spirit defies.

Through playful nudges, we craft our own tune,
With every small touch, we light up the room.
In laughter's embrace, we merrily leap,
In the softest of echoes, our bliss, we keep.

Heartbeat Beneath Our Hands

A playful push sends me tumbling down,
Your giggly laughter, my favorite sound.
With hands intertwined, we bounce with delight,
In our fool's paradise, we take flight.

A handclap that echoes, a dance of the free,
With every ambush, a shared jubilee.
Our fingers create magic, a twist and a turn,
In this comical chaos, it's love that we learn.

Waves of our friendship, like ticklish waves,
Beneath our brave hands, each other we save.
With playful jabs, and nudges so sweet,
Our heartbeat's a rhythm, with laughter to meet.

So here's to the moments that make us feel whole,
With silly handshakes that ignite our soul.
In this grand tapestry, thoughts twirling with grace,
We embrace our heartbeat, in this touch we place.

www.ingramcontent.com/pod-product-compliance
Ingram Content Group UK Ltd.
Pitfield, Milton Keynes, MK11 3LW, UK
UKHW020121171224
452675UK00014BA/1504

9 789908 012612